50 CRAZIEST BIBLE STORIES

Andy Robb

CWR

Published 2008 by CWR, Waverley Abbey House, Waverley Lane, Farnham, Surrey GU9 8EP, UK. Registered Charity No. 294387. Registered Limited Company No. 1990308. Reprinted 2009, 2010 (twice).

See back of book for list of National Distributors.

Concept development, editing, design and production by CWR

Cover image: Andy Robb

Printed in Croatia by Zrinski.

ISBN: 978-1-85345-490-5

There are some things that are really difficult to do, such as eating jelly with a pair of chopsticks, not slurping through the straw when you get to the bottom of a milkshake and keeping a straight face when someone accidentally burps in the middle of quiet reading at school. But for most people, reading the Bible tops the lot of them.

If you've never so much as taken a sneaky peek between the covers of a Bible (and even if you have), it's sometimes really head-scratchingly tricky to know where exactly to begin. For starters, the Bible isn't one big book, it's lots of smaller books (sixty-six actually) that are all crammed together like a mini-library. The books have all got fancy names, such as Genesis (which is right at the very beginning), Job (pronounced JOBE), Psalms (pronounced SARMS), Mark (which you'll be relieved to know is actually pronounced MARK), Habakkuk (which should get you a pretty good score in a game of Scrabble) and Revelation (which is right at the very end).

Just to make it even more complicated, some of the books have got more than one section (like a sort of Part One and Part Two), and each Bible book doesn't just have chapters like normal books do, it has verses as well (like you get in poems).

So, if you wanted to have a read of chapter twenty and verse seven of the second book of Kings (cos there are two of them), you may find it written like this …

2 Kings 20:7

… which, to me, looks more like a maths equation than anything to do with the Bible – but that's the way it is.

If you're itching to know what that Bible reference I just used is all about and also to find out how some perfectly good figs were (in my opinion) wasted, then you're going to need to get your hands on a copy of the Bible to check it out. In fact, you'll need a Bible to get the most out of this book, so beg, borrow or buy yourself one as soon as you can.

As it's not always easy to decide which bit of the Bible to read first and in what order you should read it, we've gone and done all the hard work for you. Aren't we kind? In this book are

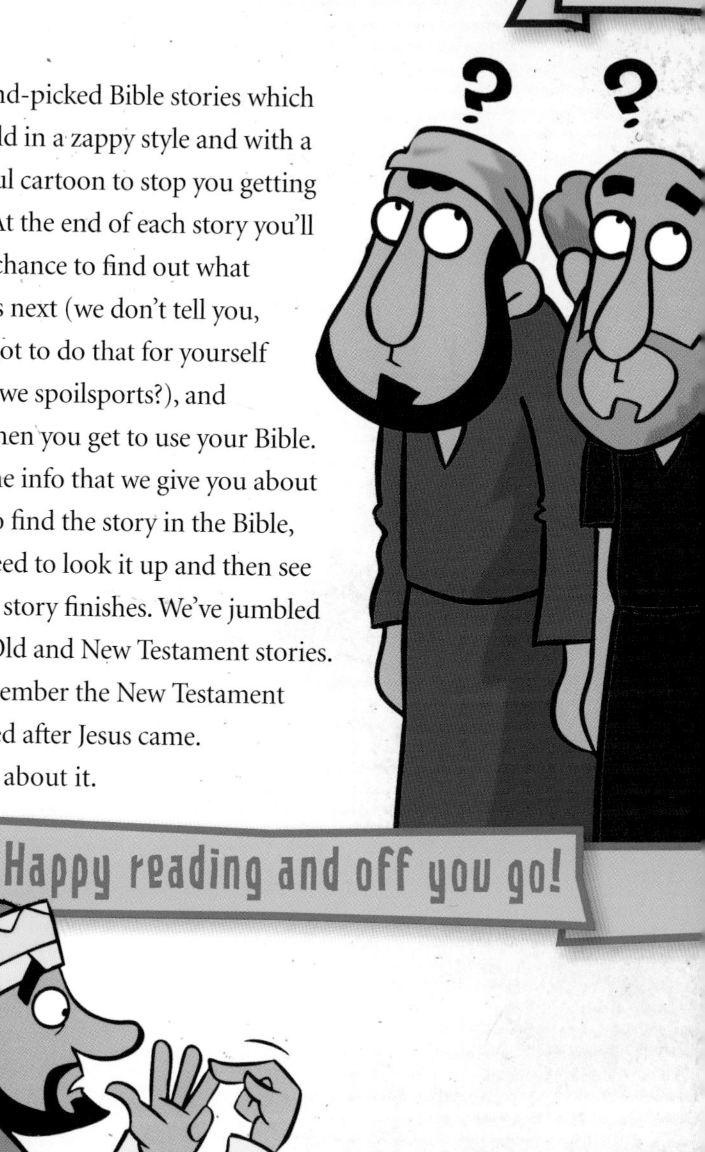

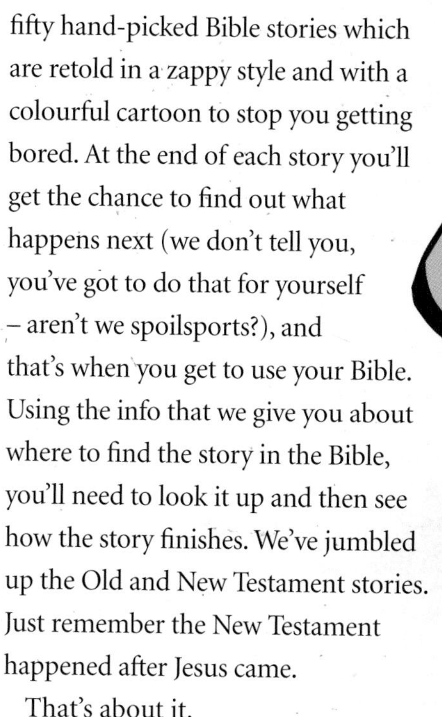

fifty hand-picked Bible stories which are retold in a zappy style and with a colourful cartoon to stop you getting bored. At the end of each story you'll get the chance to find out what happens next (we don't tell you, you've got to do that for yourself – aren't we spoilsports?), and that's when you get to use your Bible. Using the info that we give you about where to find the story in the Bible, you'll need to look it up and then see how the story finishes. We've jumbled up the Old and New Testament stories. Just remember the New Testament happened after Jesus came.

That's about it.

Happy reading and off you go!

BEDTIME 'STOREYS'

Paul was a man on a mission, haring around Europe starting churches and trying to convince people that they needed to get to know God and His Son, Jesus. It was as if Paul was making up for lost time. He'd been a Jewish religious leader for the first part of his life and had spent all his energies on torturing or locking up people who believed that Jesus was God.

All that changed when he met Jesus face to face. Now he was Jesus' biggest fan and you just couldn't shut him up – he was always blabbing about Him.

Paul was making a beeline for Jerusalem, but had stopped off for a week at Troas along the way to catch up with other followers of Jesus. On the last night of his stay, Paul and his friends were tucking into a yummy meal while Paul gave them the benefit of his wisdom. Rabbiting on was what Paul did well – and he carried on right into the night.

Paul had heaps to say before he left the next day, so he didn't bother about clock-watching (not that they had clocks in those days). Little by little, the brightly burning lamps slowly warmed the upstairs room they were using. Midnight was fast approaching and eyelids were beginning to droop. The

place must have been crammed full, because the Bible says that one of Paul's audience, a young guy called Eutychus, was perched in a window. As Paul talked on, Eutychus got sleepier and sleepier and sleepier until ... thud! Eutychus had fallen fast asleep ... and he'd also fallen out of the window. The bad news is that they were three floors up and the poor lad hit the ground with a wallop. Everyone raced downstairs, fearing the worst. Eutychus was as dead as a dodo. How's that for a rotten end to Paul's stop-off at Troas!

Well, don't jump to conclusions too quickly. All is not what it seems. Most people who fall three storeys never live to tell the tale, but this Bible bit has got the craziest ending of all.

Have a look at Bible book Acts, chapter 20 and read verses 10 through to 12 to see what I mean.

2 CATTLE BATTLE

You've probably heard of a guy in the Bible called Abram (or Abraham as God later renamed him). God had told Abram to leave Babylonia (where he lived) and to head for the land of Canaan to start a new life there. Abram was a wealthy chap in the sheep, goat and cattle department. We catch up with our main man just as he finds out he's got a sticky problem on his hands. Abram hadn't made the trek to Canaan on his lonesome. Not only had his wife and servants come along for the ride, but so had his nephew, Lot. Lot had a fair few sheep, goats and cattle of his own, and it was beginning to feel a teensy bit cramped on those Canaanite hillsides. In fact, there were so many animals grazing thereabouts that pasture land was beginning to be in rather short supply. That's when sparks began to fly.

A right old barny broke out between Abram's servants and Lot's servants about who should get first pickings of the grazing land. It was looking like a bit of a stalemate – until Abram had a bright idea. Well, to be completely honest, it actually sounds like a crazy idea, but I'll tell you what it was anyway.

Abram's solution to the cattle chaos was to part company with his nephew. They both needed more space, so it was best for everyone if they went their separate ways. Canaan was a big place and it made sense for them to spread out a bit. Instead of taking the best bit of land for himself, Lot's generous uncle let his nephew choose which part of Canaan he fancied to settle in. Lot checked out the Jordan Valley and it looked positively luscious. There seemed to be no shortage of grazing land. But Abram wasn't quite as crazy as you might think. Abram knew that wherever he went God would bless him, so he wasn't the least bit bothered that Lot seemed to have the greenest bit of Canaan for himself.

But there was another reason why Abram wouldn't touch the Jordan Valley with a barge pole. You can discover it for yourself in Bible book Genesis, chapter 13 and verses 12 and 13.

Christmas is one of my favourite times of the year. Christmas carols, roast turkey, presents under the tree. I love it all. But rewind a couple of thousand years to a place called Bethlehem and you'd soon find out that if you happened to mention Christmas, no one would have had a clue what you were talking about. Being a clever clogs, you've probably worked out why. It's because Jesus hadn't been born yet and without Jesus there isn't any Christmas.

To get you up to speed on what's been happening, Mary and Joseph (Jesus' parents) had travelled to Bethlehem and, as we catch up with them, Jesus has just been born. Jesus wasn't any old baby, He was God's one and only Son. What's even more amazing is that nobody in Bethlehem had the foggiest idea who'd been born right under their noses. But that was all about to change.

Crazy as it seems, the first people that God let in on His big secret were a bunch of common-or-garden, bog-standard shepherds. Nothing personal, fellas, I'm just saying it how it is. This was probably looking like it was going to be just another ordinary and uneventful night out on the hills around Bethlehem when, without a word of warning – BAM! – an

angel appeared. Wow, that certainly got their attention!

The shepherds were scared silly. Once the angel had calmed them down he announced the good news that a baby had been born in the nearby town and, even better, this baby was going to be the Rescuer of the world. He then suggested that they go and pay this special baby a visit. As if the shepherds hadn't had enough shocks for one night, an entire angel army then showed up, praising God and singing their hearts out to Him. What a crazy night it had been for those fellas!

Do you think they took the angel up on his offer? You can find the answer to that question by looking up Bible book Luke, chapter 2 and reading verses 15 through to 18.

Elijah the prophet had been in hiding for around about three years. Wicked King Ahab of Israel and his equally wicked wife (Jezebel) wanted him dead because he'd decreed a drought over the land. God now wanted Elijah to tell the king that he was going to send rain. King Ahab didn't exactly roll out the red carpet for God's prophet. He said that Elijah was the worst troublemaker in Israel. Elijah challenged the king to bring the 450 prophets of Baal and the 400 prophets of the goddess Asherah (whom Ahab's wife supported) to a place called Mount Carmel.

The event drew a big crowd and once everyone had assembled Elijah threw down the gauntlet: 'Make up your minds. If the Lord is God, worship Him. If Baal is God, worship him.' Elijah had two bulls brought to him: one for him and one for the prophets of Baal. They cut their bulls into pieces, put them on an altar and stacked it up with firewood. 'Pray to your god and I will pray to mine, and the one who answers by sending fire, he's God,' announced Elijah.

Elijah let the prophets of Baal have first crack of the whip and they ended up making right old fools of themselves, dancing round their altar and yelling out to their god. The

more frantic the prophets of Baal got, the more Elijah goaded them. It was pretty obvious that Baal wasn't going to come up with the goods. Elijah was beginning to enjoy this and started to taunt them that maybe their god had popped to the loo.

Next it was Elijah's turn. Elijah dug a trench around his altar, filled it full of water and then soaked the bull and the firewood until it was drenched. Elijah prayed to God that He would prove that He was Lord. Zap! Fire flamed down from heaven and burned the sacrifice to ashes, drying up the trench in the process. The onlookers were gobsmacked. They threw themselves to the ground in terror and admitted that the Lord was God.

Want to know what became of the humiliated prophets of Baal? Look it up in Bible book 1 Kings, chapter 18 and verse 40.

Naaman was a big shot in the Syrian army, but the poor chap suffered with a horrid skin disease. Fortunately for Naaman there was light at the end of the tunnel. His servant girl (who'd been captured in a raid on Israel) reckoned she knew of a guy who might just be able to help. The man she was referring to was none other than the prophet Elisha.

Naaman set off, carrying a letter from his king (addressed to Israel's king), asking for his military commander to be cured. When the king of Israel read the letter he didn't know what to do. How was he going to cure the guy? That's not the sort of thing kings do. Was the king of Syria trying to pick a fight with him?

Elisha soon got wind that the king of Israel was in a bit of a quandary and offered to help him out. Elisha had Naaman drop by at his house to see what he could do for the Syrian commander. Did Elisha wave his hand over the skin disease and make it miraculously disappear? Nope. He sent his servant out to tell Naaman to pop down to the River Jordan and wash himself seven times in the manky water. That didn't go down too well. If he'd wanted a bath they had much nicer rivers in Syria. And anyway, important people like him didn't do that sort of thing.

Naaman stormed off in a right old huff. Once his servants had calmed him down, they persuaded him to do what the prophet of God had said. Reluctantly, Naaman slunk down to the river and followed Elisha's crazy instructions. One, two, three, four, five, six, seven times he dipped himself in the Jordan.

Did Naaman's skin disease leave him or had Elisha just done it to make the Syrian commander look silly? Check out the answer in Bible book 2 Kings, chapter 5 and verses 14 to 16.

6 DAN'S DIET

How do you fancy being taken prisoner by an invading army and then whisked off to live in the land it came from? That's what happened to poor Daniel. Just when he was really beginning to enjoy his teenage years it was 'Goodbye, Judah!' and 'Hello, Babylon!' On the plus side, our Dan was a well-brought-up young lad and his privileged background helped to pull a few strings.

King Nebuchadnezzar (of Babylon) picked out all the Hebrew boys who had some sort of royal pedigree and decided to have them trained up to serve in his royal court. The king was quite a choosy chap. Not only did the young men have to be posh, but they also had to be handsome, intelligent and well-trained. Their three-year crash course in becoming a Babylonian was run by a guy called Ashpenaz, who taught them to read and write the language. To help them feel a bit more Babylonian, they were given nice new Babylonian names. From now on Daniel was known as Belteshazzar. Just to keep them in the lifestyle to which they'd been accustomed, King Nebuchadnezzar gave orders for his royal trainees to get the same tip-top quality food and drink that he tucked into every day. Looks like Daniel and his mates

had fallen on their feet … or had they?

Daniel and his fellow exiles from Judah were Jewish, which meant that they only ate certain foods allowed by God. To eat the food the king wanted to give them would have been breaking Jewish law. Daniel hit upon an idea. He and three of his mates would eat a diet of vegetables and water and nothing else. That should keep them in the clear.

Ashpenaz wasn't quite so keen on the plan. The king would kill him if the young men in his charge didn't remain fit and healthy. So Daniel then suggested to the guard appointed by Ashpenaz that he give them a ten-day trial run with the veg-and-water diet. After that he could compare them with the other young men in the royal court and see whether they looked as healthy or not. The guard reluctantly agreed to their crazy request.

Should he have been worried, or was Daniel's trust in God to keep them fit and healthy well-founded? Go to Bible book Daniel, chapter 1 and read verses 15 and 16 for your answer.

When it comes to misfits, there's none greater in the Bible than Jephthah and, yes, his name is a bit of a mouthful – so how about we call him Jeph from now on. Jeph was kicked out of his home by his half-brothers and ended up living rough in the land of Tob, hanging out with a band of no-hopers and becoming their leader. Some time later, the Ammonites decided to attack Israel (the land he'd come from) and, with that, things changed for Jeph. No longer was he 'Mr Outcast'. Suddenly, people were singing his praises for being such a great leader.

The top bods from his home town of Gilead tried to persuade him to fight with them against the nasty Ammonites. Not so fast! They'd booted him out and now they wanted him back, as if nothing had happened. It might have been flattering to be asked to lead the Israelites into battle, but Jeph wanted a return for his effort. Here's the deal he came up with. If he defeated the Ammonites, then the Israelites' part of the bargain was to make him their ruler. They agreed to Jeph's demands.

However, before our hero launched a full-scale attack on the invading Ammonite army he decided to check out why they wanted to attack Israel. He discovered that the Ammonites wanted to settle an old score against Israel. It was as simple as that. Jeph was having none of it. The Ammonites were making themselves out to be the good guys – but Jeph knew better. He told them, point blank, that Israel was on the side of right and that making war against God's special nation was one big mistake. Jeph was fired up for the fight. And then he did something really crazy. He made a promise to God: if God gave them victory over the Ammonites then he, Jeph, would sacrifice (as a burnt offering to God) the first person who came out of his house to meet him when he returned victorious.

Jeremiah was a prophet of God in Judah and his job was to pass on to the people the things that God told him to say. For his part, the king of Judah (Jehoiakim) couldn't care two hoots what Jeremiah had to say and especially if it was stuff criticising him.

God instructed Jeremiah to write down on a scroll a handy reminder of all the warnings He had given the people of Judah over the years. Jeremiah dictated the long list of stuff to his trusty scribe, Baruch, and then had him take it to the Temple to read out loud for all to hear. One of the people in earshot of Baruch was a guy called Micaiah. He reckoned that the leaders of the land needed to hear Jeremiah's message. He sped off to the royal palace and blurted out to the king's officials what he'd heard. The royal officials took their lives in their hands and handed Jeremiah's scroll to the court secretary. As a guy called Jehudi began to read from the scroll, the king did something crazy. Every time Jehudi had finished reading three or four columns the king lopped them off with a small knife and threw them into the fire.

The officials who'd made sure the king saw this scroll realised that what he was doing was wrong and desperately

tried to persuade him not to burn any more of it. Destroying a message from God was a serious thing – and King Jehoiakim ought to know it. The king couldn't have cared less. Neither he nor those close to the throne showed an ounce of remorse, in fact, the king kept on slicing up the scroll and burning it on the fire until it was all gone. Just to put the finishing touches to his crazy crime, Jehoiakim gave the order for Jeremiah and Baruch to be arrested. The good news is that they couldn't be found. But the same thing couldn't be said for the king.

If you want to find out what became of the wicked king, pick up a Bible and check out Bible book Jeremiah, chapter 36 and read verses 27 through to 32.

FORGET THE DEBT

I'll bet Peter (one of Jesus' disciples) thought he was a right old smarty pants when he asked Jesus about how many times he should forgive someone who wronged him. How about seven times? That'll make me out to be good guy. Nope! Seven times seven was Jesus' reply. In other words, just keep on forgiving and forgiving and forgiving. To make 100 per cent sure that Peter got the message Jesus told him a story to ram the point home. Here's the story.

There was a king (who represented God) who checked up on what his servants owed him. Hmm, it looked like one of them was more than a little behind with his payments – in fact, millions of pounds behind! The bottom line was that there was no way, in a month of Sundays, that this servant was going to be able to clear his ginormous debt. There was nothing for it. The king consigned the servant (and his family) to a life of slavery. The servant blubbed and begged until the king had a change of heart and forgave his whopper of a debt – lock, stock and barrel. Now here's the crazy thing.

As soon as the servant was clear of the king's palace he collared a guy who owed him a pittance and demanded that he cough up the money he owed … or else! The guy owing

money begged for time to repay his debt but … nothing doing. The servant had him chucked into jail until he settled up, but some of the other servants grassed him up to the king.

If you want to know what the king had to say about that miserly servant, you'll have to look up Bible book Matthew, chapter 18 and check out verses 32 to 35.

This Bible story is about to blow your brains with its sheer craziness. We catch up with the Israelites on their way to the land of Canaan. Along the way they'd had a squabble or two with some of the locals who didn't much like the idea of a couple of million foreigners passing through their land.

The Amorites were one such bunch. They tried to come over all tough and nasty on the Israelites but ended up with a bit of a bloody nose. Word soon got out that the Israelites were a force to be reckoned with and, to make matters worse, God was on their side. King Balak of nearby Moab didn't want to be next on the Israelites' 'hit list' so he came up with a cunning plan.

Balak sent for a prophet called Balaam and offered to pay him handsomely if only he'd rain down bucket loads of his very best curses on the Israelites. But God showed up at Balaam's place and told him not to do it. King Balak wasn't one to be put off. He kept up the pressure until Balaam eventually caved in. Balaam saddled up his trusty donkey and toddled off to meet Balak. No surprises that God wasn't pleased with Balaam for allowing his greed to get the better of him. God sent a shiny angel to stop him in his tracks but – here's the thing – the only one who could see the angel was

the donkey. The donkey was petrified and stopped dead in her tracks. There was no way she was budging an inch further with that angel blocking the path. Balaam thought his donkey was just being awkward and beat the beast to get it moving. The final straw was when the donkey, trying to avoid the awesome angel, crushed Balaam's foot against a stone wall. Balaam was hopping mad – literally! He beat the poor animal something rotten. Enough was enough. Time was moving on and Balaam wasn't about to waste it all because of a stubborn donkey.

Want to know what was crazy about this story? Well, check out Bible book Numbers, chapter 22 and scan through verses 26 to 35 to read the bizarre end to this crazy tale.

FESTERING FROGS

The Israelites had been slaves of the Egyptians for hundreds of years and they were well cheesed off about it. Being kind and caring, God sent a guy called Moses to set them free. Just one problem. The Egyptian Pharaoh was as stubborn as an ass and nothing, but nothing, was going to make him let his Israelite slaves go free.

So God instructed Moses to warn Pharaoh that if he didn't release the Israelites God would send a plague of frogs to infest the land. Nothing doing. Pharaoh wasn't going to budge, so Moses' brother, Aaron, sprang into action. He held out the special wooden staff that God had given him over the rivers, canals and pools, and up sprung frogs here, there and everywhere. Pharaoh pleaded with Moses to pray to his God to get rid of the wretched creatures and God did. When stubborn Pharaoh saw that the frogs had gone, he went back to his old ways and refused to listen to a word that Moses and Aaron said. Time for the next plague.

Aaron struck the dusty Egyptian soil with his wooden staff and this time up rose millions and millions of gnats. Ugh! They were everywhere. That'll teach Pharaoh to mess with God. But Pharaoh was spoiling for a fight. There was no way

he was going to give in now. So God sent a plague of flies. Egypt came to a complete standstill. Pharaoh summoned Moses and Aaron and offered them a compromise. He'd let the Israelites offer sacrifices to their God in the desert if Moses prayed to God to get rid of those flipping flies. They were driving him crazy. Moses agreed – but was Pharaoh a man of his word? What do you think?

Have a read of Bible book Exodus, chapter 8 and verses 30 to 32 to have your suspicions confirmed.

Most people have heard of Bible tough guy, Samson. He seemed like a crazy choice to lead the Israelite nation, but God knew what He was doing when He picked him. God wanted somebody to sort out those pesky Philistines who were forever giving the Israelites a hard time, and big, beefy Samson was the man for the job.

Samson was more brawn than brain, and he had a hot head to go with it – as this Bible story proves. Samson also had an eye for the girls and he wasted no time in getting himself a wife – only not from his own people but from the Israelites' enemies, the Philistines. Things started to go pear-shaped when Samson discovered that his father-in-law had married his wife off to another man. Samson was not a happy bunny. His father-in-law tried to palm him off with his prettier younger daughter but … Samson was having none of it.

He was one mega mad mighty man, I can tell you. He completely blew his stack and, in one crazy moment, rounded up 300 foxes, tied them together in pairs by their tails, put flaming torches in the knots and then let them loose in the Philistines' cornfields. I'll give him this – when it came to taking revenge, Samson didn't do things by halves. The terrified foxes wreaked havoc as they ran through the fields and orchards, setting them ablaze as they fled in panic. When the Philistines found out why Samson had lost his cool, they burned down his father-in-law's house and his wife's house, killing them both in the process.

13 BOY OH BOY!

I'm sure most kids would give their right arm to swap places with their school teachers for a day. Just think what fun you could have! Well, that's sort of the crazy situation Jesus found Himself in when He was only twelve years old. Actually, it's the only thing, apart from His birth, that there is in the Bible about Jesus as a youngster. It happened like this.

Once a year, Jesus' mum and dad, along with other members of the family, trekked off to Jerusalem (Israel's capital city) to celebrate the Jewish Passover Festival. After it had finished they packed their bags and headed back the way they'd come. Because they were travelling in a big group it wasn't until the end of the day that Mary and Joseph (Jesus' parents) twigged that He wasn't with them. Panic stations! They hurried back to Jerusalem to hunt for their lost lad.

It took them three whole days to track Jesus down, by which time they must have been at their wits' end. Where did they find Him? In Jerusalem's Temple, of all places. He was sitting with the religious leaders, listening to the things they had to say and quizzing them as well. One thing's for sure, Jesus had made a good impression. The religious leaders couldn't believe how smart this kid's answers were. Mary and Joseph were flabbergasted as well.

If you want to know what
Jesus had to say when His
mum told Him how worried
she'd been and asked why
He'd done this, have a look
in Bible book Luke, chapter
2 and read verses 48 to 52.
Fascinating stuff!

FORGIVE AND FORGET

Revenge is sweet, or so the saying goes, and if there's one person who seemed justified in getting his own back on someone, it was King David of Israel. When his predecessor (King Saul) discovered that David was lined up to sit on his throne and that his days as Israel's ruler were numbered, Saul gave David a hard time. In fact, King Saul became so jealous of his handsome and popular successor that he went as far as trying to kill him. Not nice!

For his part, David refused to retaliate. When Saul eventually died and David came to the throne, you could be forgiven for thinking that Israel's new king might finally seek his revenge and take it out on those of Saul's family who remained. But, crazy as it may seem, David didn't want to – because he was a man who wanted to do what was right in God's eyes. (That's actually why God chose him to be king in the first place.)

King David called for an old servant of Saul's called Ziba and asked him if any of Saul's family were still alive and kicking. Ziba piped up that he knew that one of Saul's grandsons, Mephibosheth, a lad crippled from childhood, was still around, so David sent for him. Mephibosheth bowed

down before the king, fearing the worst. The king assured Mephibosheth that all was well and that he was going to give back to him all the land that had belonged to his grandfather, Saul. How generous is that? To top it all, King David roped in Ziba, his fifteen sons and his twenty servants to farm the land and to use it to feed Mephibosheth's family. David's kindness might sound crazy to you and me, but I'll bet it sure made God happy.

King David added one more finishing touch, just to show how serious he was about letting bygones be bygones, but you're going to need to look up Bible book 2 Samuel, chapter 9 and read the second half of verse 10 to discover it.

15 GOD GOES CAMPING

One crazy-sounding thing about God is that, although He's the One who created the entire universe, He still has time for the likes of you and me. The Israelites found this out as they wandered across the desert on their way to a new place to live. They had to make do with living in tents, and what was good enough for the Israelites was good enough for God. God wanted this special nation never to forget that He was their God and that He'd always be with them.

To prove the point, God had the cream of their craftsmen build a beautiful, ornate tent for Him to live in. Just in case you're a bit confused, let me add that God was still in heaven – but because He's God that means He's able to be in more than one place at the same time.

God's tent (which was called the tabernacle) was slap-bang in the middle of the Israelite camp. Whenever the Israelites moved, so did God's tent. Because the tabernacle was God's special tent, it needed to be handled with care. That was the job of a bunch of guys called Levites. The tabernacle was the place where people went to talk to God and to make sacrifices to Him. The Bible tells us that whenever Moses (the leader of the Israelites) went to God's tent, everyone stood at a distance

to see what would happen next. Once inside, a pillar of cloud came down out of the sky and stayed at the front of the tent. It was God Himself.
God and Moses would talk face to face like good friends.

There was somebody else who spent a lot of his time in God's special tent. Head for Bible book Exodus, chapter 33 and verse 11 to find out who it was.

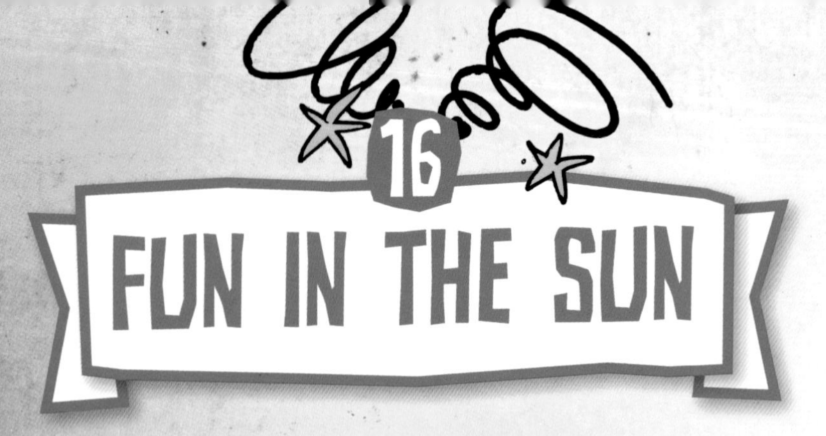

16 FUN IN THE SUN

Word had got out that the Israelites were in town. Joshua and his army were sweeping through the land of Canaan, conquering it one place at a time. With God on their side they were invincible. The Israelites had already done a pretty neat job of destroying the walled city of Jericho. They'd obliterated Ai by outmanoeuvring its fighting men, and now the mighty warriors of Gibeon had made a peace treaty with them for fear of going the same way. Adonizedek, the Amorite king of Jerusalem, had got wind of this and was none too pleased with the Gibeonites for selling out to Joshua. The people of Jerusalem were petrified of the Israelites. As far as the king was concerned, everyone should stick together and not cave in to their Israelite foe.

Adonizedek decided that the Gibeonites needed teaching a lesson. He mustered the other four Amorite kings and headed off to attack Gibeon and give them a right old walloping. When the Gibeonites found out, they quickly sent word to Joshua to come and rescue them. With his whole army in tow, Joshua set out to save the day. The Israelites had the added confidence of knowing that they were going to win the battle, hands down, because God had told them so.

The Israelites caught the Amorites off their guard. The Bible says that the Amorite army was thrown into a complete panic and was well and truly slaughtered. The terrified Amorites who escaped the sword tried to make a break for it, but the Israelites chased after them. God also rained down the biggest hailstones you've ever seen onto the fleeing Amorites and killed more of them than the Israelites had with their swords.

It was a long old battle and Joshua did something really crazy to make sure he finished the job in daylight. Find out what it was in Bible book Joshua, chapter 10 and verses 12 through to 15.

17 DIVINE DUNKER

John the Baptist had been working his socks off baptising people in the River Jordan as a sign that they wanted to wash away the bad things in their life and get a fresh start with God. John wasn't fussy about who he baptised. He'd dunk anyone. What's surprising is that people were prepared to trek all the way out into the hot and dusty desert to have this strange-looking guy give them a bath in the murky river. One person that John certainly wasn't expecting to show up was his relative, Jesus.

John was a few months older than Jesus but he'd known that there was something special about Him. John must have been scratching his head trying to figure out why on earth Jesus had dropped by. Maybe He just wanted to show a bit of interest in John's job. But that wasn't the reason. Then Jesus said something that blew John away. He wanted to be baptised by John. John simply couldn't believe his ears. No way! Jesus was God's Son. John reckoned it should be the other way round and that Jesus should be the one baptising him. But Jesus wasn't going to change His mind. He told John that this was all part of God's plan for His life and, for now, that's how it had to be – end of story.

Reluctantly, John agreed and led Jesus down into the Jordan and baptised Him. It seems that Jesus wanted to make it crystal clear that although He'd come from heaven to get the human race back to being friends with God, He wasn't going to set Himself on a pedestal. It was as if, by getting baptised, Jesus was saying that He was one of us – even though He was God. That might sound crazy – but God is always One for surprises.

God often does things in a completely different, topsy-turvy way to the way we would. The bit of the Bible we're about to check out proves my point. Let me explain.

Jesus, who in case nobody has got around to telling you (and shame on them if they haven't) is God's Son, had chosen to give up His extremely comfy life in heaven to visit planet Earth so He could patch things up between us human beings and God. Jesus' crazy-sounding plan involved getting a bunch of ordinary guys to help Him get the job done. The first men Jesus signed up to be part of His travelling band were a rag-tag group of Galilean fishermen. They might have been qualified to drop a net over the side of a boat, but what did they know about working with God? Not a lot. Anyway, here's how it happened.

Jesus was hanging out on the shore of Lake Gennesaret, teaching the crowds about God, when He suddenly stopped what He was doing and made tracks for one of the fishing boats that had been dragged up onto the beach. The fishermen were packing up after a long and unsuccessful night out on the lake, but Jesus had other ideas. Jesus told them to set sail one more time. After a bit of protesting, they pushed their boat out to sea.

Surprise, surprise! They hauled in a bumper catch, just like Jesus had promised they would. But that wasn't the end of it. Jesus told Simon, James and John that from now on it wasn't fish they'd be catching, but people. How crazy does that sound? Jesus handpicked twelve guys in all, one of whom was a cheating tax collector called Levi.

Want to know how Levi responded to Jesus' crazy offer to be one of His followers? Then look in Bible book Luke, chapter 5 and scan through verses 27 to 32.

19 HEAL DEAL

Peter and John, a couple of the main guys in the Church in Jerusalem around 2,000 years ago, were making tracks for the city's Temple. It was the middle of the afternoon and, as they approached a place called the Beautiful Gate, a beggar tried to grab their attention. The Temple area was a hot spot for beggars. It was the ideal place to prick the consciences of people who were going to worship God and to get some of their loose change. But if it was money that this particular beggar was after, then he was about to be disappointed.

Day in, day out, he held out his hand to passers-by in the hope of receiving something to live on. He had no way of earning anything because he couldn't walk. The Bible says that he had to be carried to the gate each and every day. He couldn't even get there by himself. But today, this lame beggar was in for the surprise of his life. Instead of dipping his hand into his purse and chucking the crippled beggar a coin or two, Peter looked at him, eyeball to eyeball, and said that if it was money he was after, they didn't have a bean. What they did have was the authority and power from Jesus Christ to heal sick people. And with that, Peter told the guy to get up and walk. Peter sure didn't pussy-foot around, did he? He took the man's hand and helped him to his feet. As soon as he did, the beggar's feet and ankles became strong. How crazy is that? I'll bet the beggar was glad that Peter and John had left the house without any spare cash that day.

Moving to another country to live has become really popular these days, but imagine being forced to live in another land by an invading army. That's what had happened to Ezekiel's nation, the Israelites. King Nebuchadnezzar had attacked their country and carted off most of the survivors to Babylon, where he came from.

God had actually allowed it to happen to get the Israelites' attention. They were meant to be a shining example to everyone else of how to worship God and to live God's way. Unfortunately, they were making a bit of a hash of things and were now being punished for it. On the plus side, God hadn't given up on Israel and He never would. God used prophets (guys like Ezekiel) to pass on stuff He wanted them to hear. Sometimes God even asked these prophets to do crazy things to act out what was going to happen. That's what happens in this story.

Ezekiel was minding his own business, when God gave him a strange vision that would have been a dog's idea of heaven. The vision was of a valley littered with dry bones as far as the eye could see. God told Ezekiel to talk to the bones and to tell them that He was going to put breath and life into them. He was going to give the bones sinews and muscles and cover

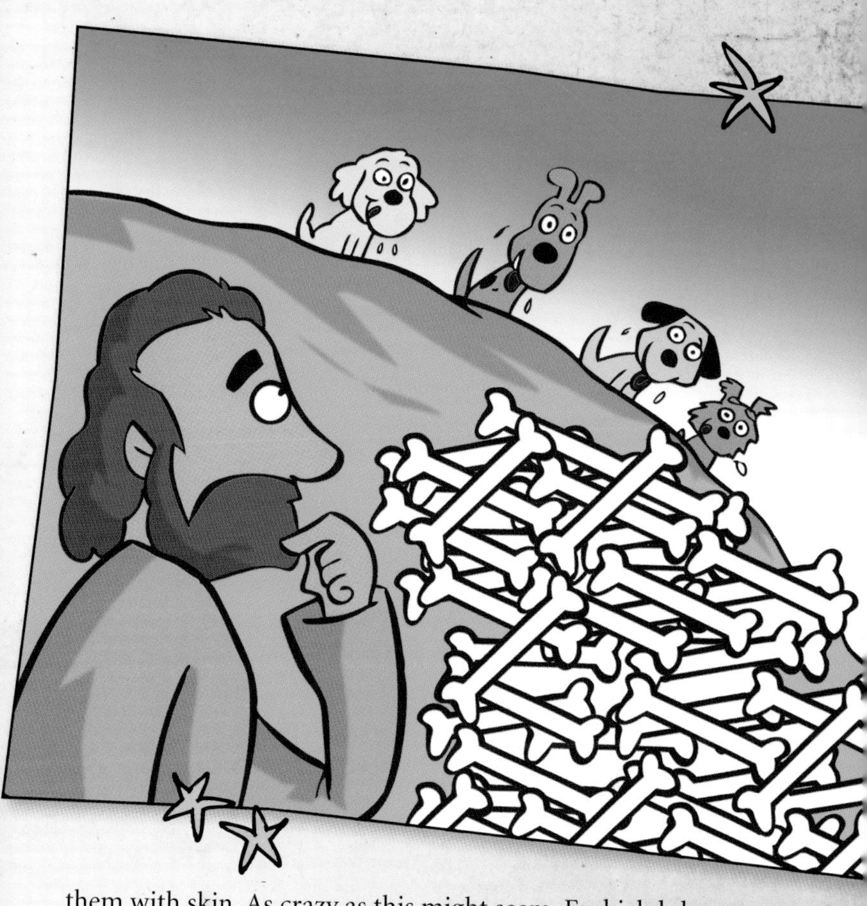

them with skin. As crazy as this might seem, Ezekiel duly obliged and – surprise, surprise – the bones started to rattle and shake as they gradually came to life again, just like God had said. Next, Ezekiel got a thumbs up from God to command the wind to breathe life back into the bodies.

Want to know what on earth all that crazy stuff was about? Get your very own finger bones moving and flick through your Bible to Ezekiel, chapter 37 and verses 10 to 14.

HEZ'S HEALING

Hezekiah (the king of Judah) was not in the best of health. Isaiah the prophet dropped by to give his ailing king a message from God: 'Get ready to die.' Not very cheery. Want to know what was making the king so poorly? The Bible says that it was all down to a boil. It must have been a bit of a biggy, that's all I can say.

Hezekiah didn't take Isaiah's message too well. He turned his face to the wall and wailed to God, reminding Him what a good king he'd been. His pleading obviously tugged on God's heartstrings. God got Isaiah to tell the king that He'd heard his prayer and seen his tears. Not only that, He was going to heal the king and give him fifteen more years of life. Hezekiah was bowled over. Phew! That was a close one. How did God heal Hezekiah? Well, to be perfectly honest, nobody's quite sure, but Isaiah had the king's attendants put a paste of figs on the boil (a waste of good figs, if you ask me) and told the king that he'd recover. That's as much as we know.

The Bible also says that God gave Hezekiah a sign that he really would get well – honest! The sign was that Hez could choose whether the shadow in the stairway of Ahaz should either go forwards ten steps or backwards ten steps. For

that to happen, the sun would have to move forwards or backwards in the sky. It seemed that God shifted everything in the universe just to convince the king that everything was going to be all right. Awesome!

Read the end of this story in Bible book 2 Kings, chapter 20 and verses 10 and 11 to see what Hezekiah chose and if God was as good as His word.

One thing that I guess most readers of this book aren't thinking about at the moment is getting married. But if you were, I'll bet you'd think twice about allowing your dad to sort out who it was you got hitched to.

Abraham was getting a bit edgy that his boy, Isaac, might end up marrying a girl who didn't worship the same God as them, so he packed his trusted old servant off to the land of Mesopotamia to fetch his lad a bride. With a herd of camels in tow, the servant headed off for the city where Abraham's brother, Nahor, lived. So far, so good.

On his arrival, the servant headed for the city well to give his weary camels a well-earned drink – and it was here that he hit upon his crazy plan. He prayed to God that if, when he asked any of the women who came to the well, 'Please, lower your jar and let me have a drink', she replied, 'Drink, and I will also bring water for your camels', he'd take that as a sign that she was the gal for Isaac. Even before the servant had a chance to say his 'Amen', a beautiful young woman showed up to collect water. Abraham's servant said his speech and – crazy or what – she gave him the right reply. Spooky! What's even more amazing is that Rebekah (the girl) was the daughter of Nahor,

Abraham's brother. What a small world it is! Everything had gone to plan. The servant knelt down with a grateful heart to give credit to God. Rebekah's family were also over the moon and it was pretty obvious to all concerned that God was behind this.

23 CHEESY CHALLENGE

You probably don't need me to tell you that Jesus wasn't just an ordinary guy. He was the Son of God, which meant that He was the most important person in the whole, vast universe and when you're that high up the pecking order you can call the shots and nobody can stop you. So, with that in mind, this bit from the Bible is going to sound all the more crazy to you.

Jesus was in Jerusalem (the capital of Israel) for the Jewish Passover Festival. It was a great time of celebration when the Jewish people remembered how God had rescued them from a life of slavery in Egypt. A lamb was sacrificed to remind them of how blood was once daubed over their doorways to protect them. This year, the Passover meant something different to Jesus because He knew that it would be the time when His life would be sacrificed for the good of all people.

As Jesus and His twelve disciples were enjoying the traditional Passover meal, He got to His feet, took off His outer garment and tied a towel round His waist. What was Jesus playing at? This sort of thing had never happened at a Passover meal before. Without a word, Jesus filled a basin with water and then headed for Peter, one of the disciples. Peter quickly

put two and two together and sussed that – shock horror – Jesus was planning to wash his feet. No way! Not Jesus. Jesus knew full well that Peter hadn't a clue what He was up to, but told him that one day he would understand the meaning of it. At which, Peter changed his mind completely and said that, all things considered, it was fine with him if Jesus did his head and hands as well while He was at it. Jesus didn't take Peter up on his offer, but it seems from what the Bible tells us about that unusual evening that Jesus eventually got round to washing the feet of every person in the room.

So why did Jesus do such a seemingly crazy thing? Check out Bible book John, chapter 13 and verses 12 through to 17 for the answer.

Peter was a big shot leader in the world's first Church (in Jerusalem), but things weren't looking good for anybody who believed that Jesus was the Son of God. King Herod didn't like followers of Jesus one itty-bitty bit! In fact, he loathed them so much he made it a hobby of his to have them put to death. One of Jesus' brothers (James) had already been run through with a sword and killed. Now it looked like Herod wanted Peter's guts for garters as well.

Peter was nabbed and thrown into jail, but Herod wasn't taking any chances. As far as the conniving king was concerned, Peter was one of the ringleaders of these Jesus people – and there was no way Peter was going to escape his clutches now that Herod had him banged up in prison. Peter had sixteen soldiers (four groups of four) to guard him and to keep their beady eyes on him round the clock.

The night before King Herod had planned to put Peter on trial, something unusual happened. Peter was fast asleep and was bound and chained, with a guard on either side and guards at the prison gates. Suddenly, a shiny angel showed up in the middle of the prison cell. He gave Peter a good old shake and told him to get a move on: to get up, get dressed

and get going. Was this for real? Peter thought he was still dreaming. This was crazy! His chains had fallen off, but the guards were oblivious to what was going on. Peter walked right out of that prison – with nobody stopping him.

As soon as Peter was a safe distance away, the angel disappeared as quickly as he'd come. Peter hurried to the house of some of his friends. They'd been praying like mad for his release and didn't quite believe it when Peter appeared at the front door. They were over the moon – but it wasn't quite such a happy ending for everyone.

Find out what I'm talking about by reading Bible book Acts, chapter 12 and verses 18 and 19.

Jesus had been arrested by Israel's religious leaders and frogmarched to the home of their high priest, a guy called Caiaphas. The place was positively heaving with religious bigwigs, most of whom hated Jesus with a passion. The religious leaders were desperately looking for something to accuse Jesus of, so that they could have Him executed – but Jesus was squeaky clean. They persuaded some people to lie about Jesus, but none of the lies held up to close scrutiny. What's crazy is that the Jewish Law these men tried to obey strictly forbade them to tell porky pies (lies), but they were so keen to be rid of Jesus that it didn't seem to bother them one little bit.

Finally, someone said something about Jesus claiming that He could tear down God's Temple and rebuild it again in three days. Yep, you're right, that does sound crazy – but Jesus wasn't talking about the great big Temple in the middle of the city. He was making a clever reference to the fact that He, God's living Temple, was going to die and then come back to life again in three days. Nobody wanted to hear His explanation though. They'd heard enough to make Him guilty in their minds. 'Are You the Messiah, the Son of God?' asked the high priest. If Jesus said, 'Yes', that's all they'd need

to accuse Him of blasphemy (which means saying something bad about God). Jesus decided it was time to blow His cover. 'So you say.' Jesus didn't stop at that and stirred them up something rotten by telling them that one day He'd also be sitting at God's side for all to see. Grrr! The religious leaders were spitting venom. They'd heard enough.

Want to know what their crazy verdict was for Jesus simply owning up to being God's Messiah? Head for Bible book Matthew, chapter 26 and look up verses 65 to 68.

26 FISH AND SHIPS

Jonah was from a place called Israel and God had given him a message to deliver to Israel's deadliest enemy, the Assyrians. God wanted to give them one last chance to mend their wicked ways. Jonah's job, as a prophet of God, was to pay a visit to Nineveh (the capital city of Assyria) and to tell them what a rotten lot they were. Easy peasy?! Not as far as Jonah was concerned. He had no intention of going within a zillion miles of Nineveh. As far as Jonah was concerned they didn't deserve to be given a last chance – and he was also just plain scared of what the Assyrians would do to him.

There was only one thing for it. Jonah scarpered. He took to his heels and ran in completely the opposite direction. He found a boat headed for Spain and jumped on board, hoping that God wouldn't notice that he'd done a runner. Our petrified prophet had forgotten one important fact about God. He can see everything. Nothing, but nothing, escapes God's eagle eyes – and that included jittery Jonah. Time to let Jonah know that God was on his case.

God stirred up the sea with a stinker of a storm, scaring the ship's crew half to death. The sailors dumped their cargo overboard to stop them sinking. But things just got worse.

Meanwhile, Jonah had taken forty winks and was oblivious to their predicament. The ship's captain was having none of that. He woke Jonah from his slumbers and told him to do something useful, like praying for their protection. When the crew cottoned on that Jonah was to blame for the storm, they chucked him overboard and it stopped.

Want to know if Jonah met a watery end? Go to Bible book Jonah (where else?), chapter 1 and read verse 17 to find out.

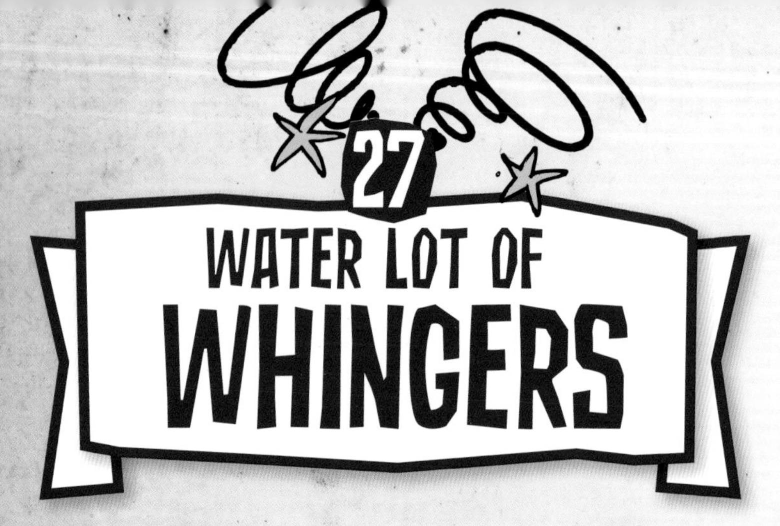

27 WATER LOT OF WHINGERS

God had rescued the Israelites from slavery in Egypt and they should have been settling down in the land of Canaan by now, if all had gone to plan. Unfortunately it hadn't – because they'd rebelled against God and were now suffering the consequences of their disobedience. This meant wandering aimlessly around a desert until all the rebels had died out. That was going to take some time, and living in a dry and dusty desert was hardly much fun. To top it all, the place where they were now camping had no water for them to drink.

They were gasping for a drink and so were their animals. As far as most of them were concerned, they felt that they'd have been better off living as slaves back in Egypt rather than dying of thirst in the desert. At least there they had enough to drink. What an ungrateful bunch of moaners and groaners they were! Not a thought for the fact that God had rescued them and then provided for them along the way. It seemed that they always had something to complain about –and God was most definitely not pleased. Nor for that matter was the Israelites' leader, Moses. Despite their ingratitude, God told Moses that He was going to give them water to drink and here's how He'd do it.

First off, Moses' brother, Aaron, had the job of getting the Israelites lined up so that they could watch what God was going to do. Next up, God told Moses to go to the rock He showed him and to speak to it. What? Yep, you heard me right. Crazy as it seems, Moses was told by God to speak to a rock and water would gush out of it.

Did Moses trust God enough to do exactly what he was told and did the Israelites get water to drink before they died of thirst? Have a look in Bible book Numbers, chapter 20 and read through verses 10 to 13.

28 SHORT-CHANGED

Being a tax collector in Jesus' day meant that just about everybody hated you. Tax collectors worked for the rotten old Romans, who ruled Israel at that time and who squeezed the Jewish population for all they could get. To add insult to injury, the sneaky tax collectors bumped up the taxes by adding on a little bit extra for themselves – cheating the people out of their hard-earned dosh. Zacchaeus was a tax collector, which makes what I'm about to tell you even more crazy. Here's what happened.

Jesus had just turned up at a place called Jericho. Whenever Jesus showed up, so did the crowds. He was a celebrity and everybody wanted to see Him. Jericho was heaving with people trying to get a slice of the action – and that included Zacchaeus. He was a short fella and wasn't going to see much if he didn't find himself a good vantage point. Just ahead of Jesus and the crowd that was following Him was a sycomore-fig tree. Zacchaeus had an idea. He raced ahead and scurried up the tree. Job done! Now he was head and shoulders above the lot of them.

As Jesus approached, Zacchaeus could see everything that was going on. Suddenly, Jesus stopped in His tracks and looked

straight up at the pint-sized pilferer. Oh no! Was Jesus going to lay into him for cheating people out of their money? If He did, the crowd would probably lynch him. Jesus didn't. Of all the crazy things, Jesus called up to Zacchaeus and told him that He was coming to stay at his house. What? He couldn't be serious! Yep, He sure was. Zacchaeus clambered down the tree, overwhelmed with joy. Nobody had ever shown kindness like that to him before. Not everybody shared Zacch's elation though. People in the crowd were well-miffed that Jesus wanted to drop in at the house of a bad person like Zacchaeus. Jesus wasn't fussed what they thought. He knew full well that even a hard-nosed cheat like Zacchaeus could change for the better.

Did he? Take a look in Bible book Luke, chapter 19 and read verses 8 through to 10 to discover for yourself.

29

KING THING

Israel had been led by a mixed bag of men (and one woman) for a few hundred years, but the Israelites were now itching for a bit of a change. Their present leader was a guy called Samuel, who wasn't getting any younger. Added to which, Samuel's two sons, Joel and Abijah, weren't exactly lining themselves up to be worthy successors to their well-respected dad. They were a couple of rogues.

The people of Israel decided to take matters into their own hands. Why couldn't Israel have a king to rule over them like every other nation? As far as Samuel was concerned, this was a complete non-starter. He really wasn't happy with the idea one bit. Israel didn't need a king to rule them. That was God's job. Samuel went away and prayed to God about it.

What was God's answer? He told him to give the Israelites what they wanted and blow the consequences. If it was a king they wanted, then give them a king. God reminded Samuel that they had always been a rebellious people – and rejecting God as their King was just more of the same. God also told Samuel to warn them that if they did get a king he'd make soldiers of their sons; their sons would end up ploughing the king's fields (not their own); their daughters would end up

working for the king as perfumiers, cooks and bakers; he'd nab their best fields, vineyards and olive groves and give them to his officials; he'd take a tenth of their corn and grapes for his royal courtiers; he'd take their servants and their best cattle and donkeys; he'd take a tenth of their flocks; and to top it all they themselves would end up as the king's slaves.

As if that wasn't enough, God also said that when all this did actually happen and the Israelites realised what a big boo boo they'd made, He wouldn't listen to their moans and groans. It would be tough luck!

Did Israel get a king? Find out in Bible book 1 Samuel, chapter 8 and verses 21 and 22.

30 LAST, BUT NOT LEAST

King Saul (of Israel) was making a bit of a hash of being the country's ruler, so God decided to call time on his reign. God sent the prophet Samuel to hunt out Saul's successor in a little town called Bethlehem (which you've probably heard of in another well-known Bible story). Samuel was a bit of a big shot in Israel, so when he showed up in town the city leaders were scared stiff in case they'd done something to offend God. Samuel soon quelled their fears and filled them in on what he was there for. But before Samuel got stuck into the business of finding Israel's next king he suggested that a sacrifice be made to God and that local man Jesse and his sons take part, which they did. Then Samuel got going with his hunt for a king.

First up was Jesse's son, Eliab. He was tall. He was handsome. Hmm, a definite possibility. But God didn't think so and reminded Samuel that He couldn't care less what someone looks like. The only thing God's interested in is a person's heart – and whether or not they love and obey Him. Next in line was Abinadab, then Shammah, but they were no good either. Samuel worked his way through all seven of Jesse's sons but God gave each of them the thumbs down. Just before Samuel gave it up as a bad job he thought to ask if Jesse had any more sons – as if seven wasn't quite enough for any man. The answer was a surprising 'yes'. David, the kid brother, was out looking after the sheep – but surely God wouldn't be interested in a young lad like him? Or would He?

31 LOLLY FOLLY

Most of us love a good story – and Jesus knew that when He taught people about God. All the stories Jesus told had a meaning, so when, one day, He launched into a tale about a dad and his two sons, people would have been all ears, trying to guess what the point of it was. Here's how it went.

The younger of the dad's two lads had itchy feet and wanted to spread his wings and travel the world. He wasn't prepared to wait for his share of what was coming his way when his dad died. He wanted the cash now! The dad agreed to his request, and off the son headed to spend his share of the loot. While he was out of the country he lived it up big time until, suddenly, it was all gone. The young man was penniless and, to make matters worse, the land he was living in was hit by a famine. Things weren't looking too rosy. He managed to find himself a job feeding pigs, but got paid next to nothing and couldn't even afford the money for some nosh of his own. He'd well and truly hit rock bottom – and he knew it.

What a botch he'd made of things! There was only one thing for it. The lad headed for home, with his tail between his legs, hoping that, just maybe, his dad might give him a job as a hired hand. Jesus was telling this story to show how we've all gone off the rails and need to return to our heavenly Father – God.

Did the dad in the story read his son the riot act? Take a look in Bible book Luke, chapter 15 and read verses 20 to 24 to find out how God treats people who come back to Him after they've done wrong.

32 BEAN STEW-PID

This Bible story stars a couple of brothers. In fact, they were twins and, as you're about to find out, this meant double trouble!

Even while they were still in their mum's tum this terrible twosome just wouldn't stop tussling with each other. It was beginning to wear their mum (Rebekah) down. 'Why me?' she wailed to God. He told her that it was because both boys would one day give birth to a nation – but the pair of them would be forever at each others' throats. How comforting was that for a mum-to-be? God also added that the elder twin (Esau) would end up serving the younger twin (Jacob).

Fast forwarding a bit, Esau grew up to be an outdoor type, but Jacob was a stay-at-home sort of guy. One day, while Esau was out risking life and limb looking for wild animals to kill, Jacob was back home cooking dinner. Suddenly Esau returned, barging into the kitchen and demanding some of Jacob's stupendous stew! He was famished! Not so fast, thought Jacob, always looking for a cunning way to get one over on his big brother. 'Tell you what,' Jacob said, 'you can have some stew on one condition. Give me your rights as the eldest son and the food's yours, bruv.' Well, that's not quite how the Bible puts it, but you get the idea.

Did Esau sell out for a measly bowl of his brother's broth? Look up Bible book Genesis, chapter 25 and read verses 31 to 34 to find out.

The Israelites had escaped from slavery in Egypt and were headed for a brand-new homeland called Canaan, hand-picked for them by none other than God Himself. After years and years of suffering at the hands of their Egyptian masters you'd think that the Israelites would be clicking their heels with joy at being free. Not so! The Israelites were well and truly miffed about the daily desert diet and they wasted no time in giving their leader (Moses) an earbashing with their complaints. The bottom line is that the Israelites figured they'd have been better off dead in Egypt rather than dying of starvation in the desert they were crossing. How's that for gratitude?

The Bible makes it clear that God wasn't too happy about the way the Israelites were behaving: all it did was to demonstrate their complete lack of trust in Him. Hadn't they grasped the fact that if God had rescued them from Egypt, He was hardly going to let them die in the desert? Hello?

Being kind and generous, God promised them as much food as they could eat, morning, noon and night. And God was as good as His word. That evening the most ginormous flock of quails (nice, meaty birds) you've ever seen flew in and covered

the camp. Let's hope the Israelites didn't stuff themselves silly, because next morning breakfast turned up in the form of a thin, flaky substance that covered the desert floor like dew. It was as delicate as frost and sweet to taste. God had come good for them once again. When the Israelites saw this crazy-looking food they asked an obvious question: 'What is it?' This is why it ended up getting called *manna* which means – yes, you've guessed it – 'What is it?' Each person could collect up to two litres of manna a day, max, but that was it. On top of that, nobody was allowed to stash any of the manna away until the next day.

Take a quick look at Bible book Exodus, chapter 16 and verse 20 to find out if everybody took God's advice.

34 WIVES, WIVES, WIVES

Most people would be content to have just the one wife, but the main man in this Bible story stacked up a staggering seven hundred. Yes, you heard me right. Seven hundred! He was none other than King Solomon of Israel (the son of King David).

King Solomon started out really good as Israel's king, and all seemed to be going well until his great wealth and power got the better of him. God had laid it on the line to the king that no way was he to take a wife from any of the nations that surrounded Israel. That's not because He thought they were ugly or even that they weren't nice people. The problem was that these other nations didn't worship the God of Israel. They worshipped their own made-up gods such as Astarte, Chemosh and Molech. God wasn't one to mince words. He called them 'disgusting'. If Solomon got hitched to a foreign wife she'd end up bringing her minging gods into Israel and that was a non-starter as far as God was concerned.

Did King Solomon heed God's warning? Nope! He not only completely ignored it but he went all out for the world record for having the most foreign wives. Solomon not only took a humungous seven hundred wives but he also had three hundred concubines (unofficial wives) to make it up to a round one thousand. Just think of all those wedding anniversaries he'd have to remember.

God knew what He was talking about when He warned Solomon of the dangers of taking foreign wives. It wasn't long before the king was worshipping their gods himself and he even sank so low as to build places of worship for them. God was miffed with His king and even showed up twice to tell him so – but Solomon simply wouldn't listen.

Jacob had been away from home for a few years but he was finally heading back to the land of his birth. He'd originally left to escape the wrath of his big brother (Esau), whom he'd double-crossed. Now it was his Uncle Laban he was running from.

God had hand-picked Jacob to head up a special nation of people who would show others who God was and how much He loved them. Couldn't God have found somebody better than Jacob? I suppose He could have done – but God specialises in taking ordinary people and making them extraordinary. Jacob knew he'd fouled up, but he still wanted to trust God and do whatever God wanted. God was about to give our main man a second chance. Before Jacob reached home, he needed time out with God to work a few things through.

In the dead of night, as Jacob was all alone, a man appeared as if from nowhere. Was he an angel from God or was this God Himself? Whoever he was, he started wrestling with Jacob. Jacob wasn't having any of that – and fought back. The two of them scrapped right through the night. What was going on? As the night wore on and the fight continued, Jacob became even more determined. He'd had enough of living on his wits. He figured it was time to live life God's way, and to do that he needed God's blessing. He wasn't going to let go of this guy, whoever he was, until he got it. As they tussled and tugged, the man from God asked a strange question. He asked Jacob what his name was. He then told Jacob that because he'd fought well and won, he was going to have a new name. It was 'Goodbye, Jacob' and 'Hello, Israel'. Jacob's life would never be the same again – and for another important reason.

Egypt's Pharaoh had just woken up from a grotty night's sleep. He'd had a couple of disturbing dreams that had really put the wind up the world's most powerful man. He sent for his magicians and wise men to see if any of them could tell him what his crazy dreams meant.

Pharaoh's heart sank as, one by one, the magicians and wise men told him that they hadn't the foggiest idea. Just as Pharaoh was beginning to despair, his wine steward had a bright idea. He'd suddenly remembered that there was a Hebrew slave called Joseph with whom he'd once shared a prison cell. This Hebrew guy had interpreted a dream he'd once had – so he was worth a try.

Joseph was whisked off to see the waiting Pharaoh but quickly made it clear that it wasn't because of any cleverness on his part that he could interpret dreams. It was a gift that God had given him.

Now for the dreams. In the first one, Pharaoh had dreamt that he was standing at the edge of the River Nile (in Egypt) when seven fat cows came out of the river and started munching on the grass. They were quickly followed by seven skinny cows who joined the fat ones on the river bank. The

skinny cows tucked into the fat cows and gobbled them all up.

In the second dream there were seven full and ripe ears of corn growing on one single stalk. Then seven more ears of corn sprouted but these were thin and weak. They swallowed up the full ones. Joseph explained that both dreams meant the same thing. The fat cows and the full ears of corn represented seven years of good harvests throughout the land. The skinny cows and the thin ears of corn represented seven years of famine. The dreams were God's way of warning the Egyptians that they were going to enjoy seven bumper years followed by seven years of famine.

Did Pharaoh pack Joe back off to prison once he'd done his stuff? Find out what became of Joseph right after he'd interpreted the dreams by going to Bible book Genesis, chapter 41 and look up verses 33 to 41.

The Midianites had been giving the Israelites a bit of a hard time, but only because God had allowed it. If only they'd stuck to worshipping Him and not the gods of the land they lived in, then everything would have been hunky-dory. God took pity on the Israelites when they begged Him for help and He raised up a leader to defeat their oppressors. Who did God pick for the job? None other than a rather insecure guy called Gideon.

Gideon was busily threshing wheat, when he had an unexpected visit from an angel who addressed him as 'brave and mighty man!' Come on! Get real! Anybody, especially God, would know that Gideon wasn't either of those things. But the angel informed Gideon that he was God's choice to be the Israelites' main man to lead them to victory. Gideon must have thought that the angel was out of his mind. It was a crazy notion. How was someone like puny him going to rescue Israel? His clan was the weakest in the tribe of Manasseh and, to make matters worse, he was the least important member of his family. As far as Gideon was concerned, he was bottom of the pile. If this really was from God, Gideon was going to need some convincing.

Gideon needed some time to think, so he cooked the angel a tasty stew while he mulled things over. The angel nearly scared the pants off Gideon when he reached out and touched the bread and meat with his stick – and burned them to a cinder in an instant. Whoa! This really was God. Gideon was now fired up to lead his people to victory. With God as his strength, Gideon was ready for action. He blew the trumpet to call his troops to war. And then, at the eleventh hour, Gideon suddenly appeared to get cold feet. He needed to check this out one last time.

Take a look in Bible book Judges, chapter 6 and skip through verses 36 to 40 to discover Gideon's completely crazy idea to make absolutely sure that he was God's man for the job.

NOW YOU SEE HIM

The Roman rulers of Israel had executed Jesus by nailing His body to a wooden cross and leaving Him there until He died. Jesus' body was then laid to rest in a tomb. This had all happened on the Friday, but it was now Sunday.

Two of Jesus' followers (Mary and Mary Magdalene) wanted to pay their last respects to Him but they'd had to wait until the Jewish Sabbath had passed. They turned up at the tomb armed with spices to cover Jesus' dead body. Just one problem. Someone had rolled a stone in front of the entrance to the tomb. The two ladies weren't going to be able to shift that humungous rock in a month of Sundays. The spoilsport Romans had also posted soldiers outside the tomb just to make sure that nobody nicked Jesus' body. Rumours had circulated that Jesus was going to come back to life again, and if that happened it would be rather embarrassing for the Romans.

One thing nobody had bargained on was God getting involved. That was the last thing they needed. Tough! Being stuck in a tomb wasn't part of the plan for God's one and only Son. Just to prove it, God dispatched a shiny angel to scare the pants off the Roman soldiers. It certainly did the trick! One

look at the awesome being was all it took to make them keel over with fright. While the guards cowered in the corner, the angel casually rolled the whopper of a stone away to reveal the entrance to the tomb. The angel was well aware of why the women had dropped by and broke the news to them as best he could – Jesus wasn't there any more. He made them take a peek inside the tomb and – guess what – no Jesus.

What had happened to Jesus? Scurry off to Bible book Matthew, chapter 28 and check out verses 5 through to 10 for your answer.

The Israelites were camping at the foot of Mount Sinai and Moses, their leader, had disappeared up it to meet up with God. As time wore on the Israelites began to wonder where on earth Moses had got to. Perhaps he'd gone off and left them. What sort of leader was that?

They quickly collared Moses' brother (Aaron) and gave it to him straight: 'We don't know what's become of this Moses who led us out of Egypt, so make us a god to lead us.' Aaron caved in to their demands and got the people to bring all their gold earrings to him. If they wanted a god, then a god he'd give them. Aaron melted down the earrings and poured the molten gold into a mould, fashioned to look like a gold bull-calf. When the Israelites saw the finished thing they crazily declared that this was the god who'd led them out of Egypt. As if! To add insult to injury, Aaron built an altar in front of the golden calf and announced that the next day there was going to be a festival to honour the Lord. Hang on a minute! This is doubly crazy. That gold bull-calf isn't the Lord God – it's just a lump of gold.

The people were up bright and early the next day to bring their sacrifices to the statue. God was furious and told Moses

that He was going to wipe the lot of 'em off the face of the earth. Moses begged God to change His mind and amazingly He did. Moses hotfooted it down the mountain, as fast as his ageing legs would carry him, to find out if things were as bad as God said they were. Moses was carrying a couple of stone slabs on which God had carved important rules that He expected the Israelites to abide by. When Moses caught sight of the Israelites whooping it up and worshipping the gold bull-calf, he was well mad.

He flung the stone slabs angrily to the ground, smashing them to smithereens.

To find out what other crazy thing Moses did, take yourself to Bible book Exodus, chapter 32 and check out verse 20.

Peter had spent the past three years as one of Jesus' disciples and life with Him was exciting. Everyone seemed to love Jesus except, that is, the religious leaders who were teeth-gnashingly jealous of God's Son. Suddenly, Peter's world had come crashing down around his ears. His master had just been arrested by those scheming religious leaders and – what now? One minute Jesus was teaching the adoring crowds about God and healing the sick, and the next He was on trial at the home of the Jewish high priest.

Peter was lurking in the shadows outside, trying to find out what had become of Jesus, when one of the high priest's servant girls accused him to his face of being something to do with Jesus. Peter was caught off guard and denied it, point blank. Imagine, after all the time he'd spent with Jesus, pretending that he didn't know Him. How crazy is that? You can't go around disowning your friends just to protect your own skin. But that's precisely what Peter was doing. To add insult to injury, Peter swore that he didn't know who Jesus was not once, but three times. I can only guess that he must have been so scared stiff of getting arrested himself that he'd spout out almost anything to get himself off the hook.

Sad to say, Jesus had actually warned Peter that he'd do this and that it would happen before the cock crowed.

The past three years had been a bit of a whirlwind for Jesus' disciples. Jesus had plucked them out of their humdrum lives to become His followers and to learn to do the things He did. It all came to an abrupt end when Jesus was put to death by Israel's Roman rulers.

Then, three days later, Jesus came back to life, before returning to heaven a few weeks after that. Of all the crazy-sounding things, Jesus had gone and left this motley bunch of disciples in charge of carrying on His work of telling people about God and demonstrating that God loved them. But how were they going to do that? Jesus was God. They were just ordinary people. Jesus had already thought of that and had instructed them to wait in Jerusalem for something that would give them all the power they'd ever need. What was this special thing? I'll tell you. It was the Holy Spirit.

Once Jesus was back in heaven, the plan was for Him to send the Holy Spirit to live in His followers. The Holy Spirit brings God's power and life and with Him living inside them they'd be unstoppable. So, Jesus' followers were hanging out in Jerusalem, waiting for what Jesus had promised them. Jerusalem was heaving with visitors who'd come to celebrate

the Jewish festival of Pentecost. Suddenly, as if from nowhere, the whooshing noise of a mighty wind filled the room. It was God's Spirit announcing His arrival. As if that wasn't enough proof that God was in the house, something that looked like tongues of fire fell on each of their heads. Fear not! They didn't get singed scalps. This wasn't real fire, just the Holy Spirit's way of making an appearance. The Bible tells us that everyone was filled with the Holy Spirit. That meant that God was now living inside them. How crazy does that sound? But God wasn't finished with this bunch of bowled-over believers. When they started to talk it wasn't their native Galilean language they spoke.

Want to know what language these Holy Spirit-filled followers began to blurt out? Take a look in Bible book Acts, chapter 2 and have a scan through verses 5 to 11.

Paul and Barnabas were in the Mediterranean town of Lystra where they were busily teaching people about Jesus. Paul noticed that one guy in the audience was hanging on his every word. The man in question had been a cripple from birth and Paul, not one to miss an opportunity to introduce someone to God's healing power, looked the man squarely in the eye and ordered him to stand up. He didn't need telling twice. The man leapt to his feet. He could walk.

Instead of God getting the credit for the miracle, the locals whipped themselves up into a frenzy and declared that Paul and Barnabas must be gods – because who else could heal a man like that? They gave Barnabas the name of the god Zeus and Paul the name of the god Hermes. That wasn't the end of it. The priest of the god Zeus in Lystra brought bulls and flowers to our troubled twosome to offer as sacrifices. Things weren't going the way Paul and Barnabas would have liked. There was only one thing for it. Something had to be done to stop this craziness as quickly as it had begun. Paul and Barnabas ripped their clothes (as a sign of sorrow) and rushed into the crowd, trying to convince the chaotic gathering that they weren't gods but simply ordinary, run-of-the-mill human

beings like the rest of them. But the Lystrans were having none of it. Then, right in the middle of the commotion, a posse of Jews from Antioch and Iconium showed up and wasted no time in setting the crowd against Paul and Barnabas.

What a turnaround! Take a look in Bible book Acts, chapter 14 and read verses 19 and 20 to find out what they ended up doing to poor Paul.

43 TIP-TOP TIPPLE

Jesus, God's one and only Son, was no ordinary person, but for thirty years He'd lived an ordinary life as a carpenter in a place called Nazareth (in Israel). At long last, the time had come for Jesus to step up to the plate and to show Himself for who He really was.

A few days earlier, Jesus had been baptised in the River Jordan by a guy called John the Baptist who was totally clued up about who Jesus was. Next up, Jesus had hand-picked a team of men (His disciples) to help Him with His mission to tell people about God. Jesus, His mum and His trusty disciples were now partying at a wedding in a place called Cana but – look out – something crazy is about to happen.

Slap-bang in the middle of the festivities the wine ran out. That's what I call bad timing. Jesus' mum decided to get involved and had a word with her Son about the predicament. She told Him to do something – pronto! By all accounts she wasn't prepared to take no for an answer. Jesus spied six one-hundred-litre water jars that were used for ritual washing. They'd do! Jesus instructed the servants to fill 'em up with water and then deliver the jars to the guy in charge. But when he took a sip, it wasn't water he tasted, but wine. Yep, sounds crazy, but wine it was. Jesus had miraculously turned the water into wine. The servants must have been gobsmacked, but the wedding organiser had no idea that a miracle had happened right under his nose. Not only was it wine, but there was also something special about it.

The Philistine army had just taken a right old hammering from their archenemies, the Israelites. King Saul of Israel had been so keen to make sure of his army's victory that he swore a crazy oath: anybody who ate anything before he'd got his revenge on the Philistines would be under a curse. It didn't help their hunger when they stumbled across a wooded area, chock-a-block full of honey.

King Saul's son (Jonathan) was blissfully unaware of his dad's oafish oath and just went right ahead and scoffed the scrummy honey. Jonathan was amazed when he discovered his dad's crazy curse. He reckoned that the Israelites could have killed even more of the Philistines if they'd been well fed. With their tums rumbling, the Israelite army went back into battle, but by the end of it they were so hungry that they started slaughtering the Philistines' sheep and cattle. When Saul found out, he was actually more concerned about the fact that they were eating meat with the blood of the animal still in it (something Jewish law strictly forbade). Saul stopped their battlefield barbecue in its tracks and set up a stone altar to kill the animals properly.

Job done, Saul was spoiling for a bit more action. He rather liked the idea of a surprise night-time attack on the

Philistines, but decided that it might be a good idea to see what God had to say on the matter first. But God wasn't saying anything. How come He was so tight-lipped? Saul figured that God's silence must mean that someone among them had sinned. It soon became all too clear that Jonathan was the culprit. However crazy the king's curse was, God held Saul to his words. Jonathan came clean and admitted he'd scoffed some honey and told his dad to go ahead and kill him if he so wished. Well, like it or not, King Saul was up for it. Some dad!

Was it a happy ending for Jonathan, or did his honey snack cost him dear? Hurry along to Bible book 1 Samuel, chapter 14 and read verse 45 for your answer.

If I told you that 300 men could defeat an army of 135,000 you'd think I was stark raving bonkers, but you'd be wrong. The star of this Bible story is a guy called Gideon. You may remember God had given him the job of leading the Israelite nation, who'd been having a spot of bother with the Midianites. They were making the Israelites' lives a misery, destroying their crops and nicking their cattle. God wanted Gideon to put a stop to it. Reluctantly he agreed.

As Gideon positioned his army south of the Midianite camp, God unexpectedly decided to make a last-minute change to the Israelite team line up. He told Gideon that if his 32,000-strong fighting force did manage to knock the Midianites for six, they'd take all the credit. That wouldn't do – so God made Gideon send home everyone who was afraid. A whopping 22,000 scaredy cats packed their bags and beat a hasty retreat home. What was God doing? This was crazy. That left only 10,000 against the Midianites' 135,000.

Next up, God instructed Gideon to take his band of men down to the water's edge for a drink. Most of Gideon's soldiers lapped up the water with their tongues, like a dog. God told Gideon to send this lot home as well. Guess how many that

left? Well you don't have to, I'll tell you. It was a measly 300. Yep, that's right 300! God had left Gideon with just 300 men to fight against the mega-massive Midianite army. You think that's crazy – well wait until you hear about God's plan of attack! He made Gideon split his barmy army into three groups of 100 and give each man a trumpet and a jar with a blazing torch inside it. They surrounded the Midianite camp in the dead of night, and on Gideon's signal all 300 of them blew their trumpets and broke the jars they were holding. The sleepy Midianites were thrown into a complete panic, with all the commotion and the bright lights.

But if you want to discover how this crazy story ended, then you'll need to hurry to Bible book Judges, chapter 7 and look up verses 22 through to 25.

46 WARY MARY

Mary, the star of this Bible bit, lived in the out-of-the-way town of Nazareth and was lined up to be married to a guy called Joseph. The chances are she was still just a teenager – which made what happened next even more surprising.

A shiny and powerful angel from God showed up, completely unannounced. 'Peace be with you!' was the angel Gabriel's opener. I don't know whether that made Mary feel a whole lot easier, but the angel just kept on with his message from God. He told a rather stunned Mary that God was with her and that He'd blessed her, big time. What on earth had she done to catch the eye of God? It didn't seem to make sense. Why would the God who made the entire universe be interested in an ordinary girl from an ordinary town in the back of beyond? It was crazy. She was bamboozled. While Mary's mind was working overtime trying to figure out what was going on, the angel Gabriel spilled the beans.

The bottom line was this. God was planning to send His Son (Jesus) to planet Earth as a human being. So far, so good. Which meant that Jesus was going to need to be born the normal human way. If you know a thing or two about biology, you'll know that would involve Him having a human mum. I'm sure by now you've put two and two together and worked out that this was the purpose of the angel's unannounced visit. It was to tell Mary that she was going to be the mum of God's Son. Wow! The angel told Mary that her child was going to be the most powerful and important person who ever lived and that His influence would just roll on and on, forever and ever. But, hang on a minute! Mary wasn't married yet. How was she going to have a baby without her hubbie-to-be getting involved? Good question – and that's exactly what Mary was thinking as well.

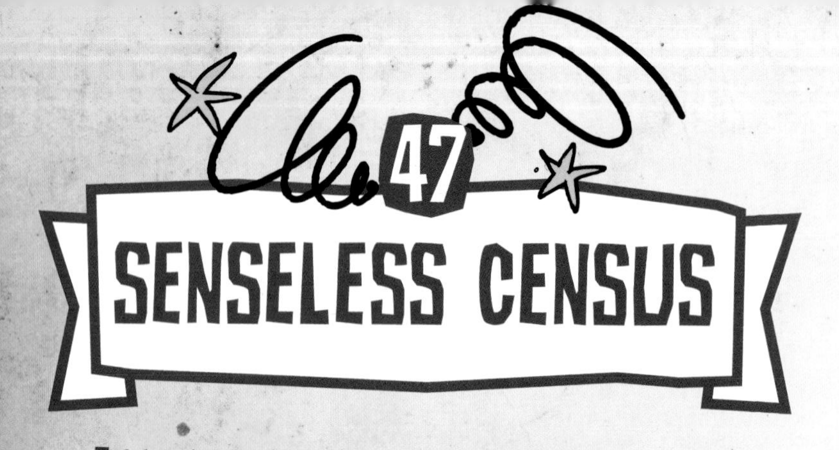

SENSELESS CENSUS

If there's one thing that makes God happy, it's people who trust Him. King David of Israel was one such man, but in this particular Bible story he's having a bit of an off day. Whenever the Israelites went to war, it wasn't the size of their army that was meant to give them the victory but the fact that God was on their side. So, when King David hit upon the idea of doing a bit of a count up of how big his army was, God was none too pleased. If the king started to get his kicks from the size of his army, he'd stop relying on God – and that was a bad move.

It wasn't only God who knew that taking a census was a mistake. Joab, the commander of Israel's army, also had alarm bells ringing in his head and he told King David as much. Joab figured that God could make their army a hundred times bigger if He wanted, but doing a head count was not a good idea. Sad to say, King David crazily completely ignored Joab's wise advice and went ahead with the census.

To David's credit, as soon as the count up was finished, he realised what a boo boo he'd made – but by then it was too late. God was going to punish the Israelites because of their king's lack of trust in Him. The Bible tells us that God gave

King David three choices of punishment. Three years of famine, three months of running away from their enemies or a three-day plague. Hmm! Tricky one that. None of them looked that clever. David plumped for the three-day plague. It killed 70,000 people and would have done even more damage if God hadn't called a halt to it.

To find out what King David had to do to keep it that way, head for Bible book 2 Samuel, chapter 24 and look up verses 18 to 25.

Often as not, Jesus was on the road, crisscrossing Israel telling people about God and healing the sick. Jesus didn't go it alone; He had twelve trusty disciples to share the load, plus heaps of other friends and supporters who kept Him fed and watered. Lazarus and his two sisters, Mary and Martha, were part of that group. The three of them lived in a place called Bethany.

As we dive into this Bible story, Jesus has just arrived at their house for a spot of dinner. Jesus was on His way to Jerusalem, and I'll bet He was ready for a well-earned breather. Jesus' disciples were well aware that His visit to Jerusalem was more than just a sightseeing trip. He'd already told them that He was going to have to suffer and die at the hands of men. Could this be when that was going to happen?

One of the two sisters (Mary) must have sensed that Jesus was up to something. As soon as dinner was served, Mary fetched a half-litre container of pure nard and poured it on Jesus' feet. Next, she knelt down and wiped Jesus' feet with her hair. The Bible says that the whiff of the perfume filled the whole house – or words to that effect. Nard might sound a bit like lard, but it was nowhere near as cheap or commonplace.

It was a mega-expensive perfume that cost the equivalent of almost a year's wages for a farm worker in those days – which makes it a jolly pricey thing to be pouring away so liberally. One of Jesus' disciples (Judas, their treasurer) thought so and ripped into Mary for wasting this top-of-the-range smelly. He figured that it would have been a much better thing to have flogged it and given the money to the poor.

Did Jesus agree with him? Nope! Jesus actually defended her crazy actions.

So what was Mary up to? Did she know something that Judas didn't? Have a look at Bible book John, chapter 12 and read through verses 7 and 8 to make an interesting discovery.

Jacob was doing a runner. He'd double-crossed his big brother Esau and was now looking for a bolt hole, out of harm's way. The place he was headed was the home of his uncle Laban in faraway Mesopotamia. His uncle was pleased to see his long-lost nephew and soon made him feel at home.

Jacob didn't want to sponge off his uncle, so he offered to help out with Laban's flocks. Uncle Laban must have been in a pretty good mood that particular day because he refused to allow Jacob to work for nothing. 'Name your price, nephew.' Jacob had a good old ponder. What to suggest as his asking price? Well, his uncle did have two daughters and the younger of the two was certainly a bit of a looker. The truth of the matter is that Jacob had fallen for his younger cousin – hook, line and sinker. He was smitten. Jacob offered to work for Laban for seven years in return for the hand of Rachel in marriage.

Laban agreed. It was a done deal. The Bible says that the seven years seemed like just a few days to lovestruck Jacob. Finally, the big day arrived. Laban threw a whopper of a wedding feast and invited anybody and everybody. Now here's where it goes crazy. That night, instead of going home with Rachel as his wife, Laban rigged it so that Jacob got landed with the less attractive Leah instead. How rotten is that! Poor Jacob didn't find out that he'd been duped until next morning – and by then it was too late.

When Jesus was alive on earth He usually had a big crowd of people following Him around wherever He went. 'Why's that?' you ask. It's because Jesus showed people how much God loved them by healing them and teaching them about God in a way that they could get to grips with.

All that non-stop teaching and healing was tiring stuff, and Jesus and His disciples figured that they were due for a well-earned break. They sailed across Lake Galilee, away from the crowds, and made for a nice, quiet place. Or so they thought! Word soon got out where Jesus and His team were headed and what was meant to be a relaxing getaway turned into yet another open-air meeting. The Bible helpfully informs us that there were five thousand men who'd caught up with Jesus – so you could probably easily double that number if you added women and kids.

Jesus asked one of His team (a guy called Philip) if he had any bright ideas about how they were going to feed everyone. Jesus figured that the crowd would be famished after traipsing around all over the place, but what were they going to do? McDonald's hadn't been invented yet and, even if it had, Philip reckoned it would cost a small fortune to cover the bill.

Any other suggestions?

Andrew, another of Jesus' team, said there was a kid with a packed lunch. Well, actually it was only five small barley loaves and a couple of fish. That was hardly going to feed a hillside full of people, but I suppose it's the thought that counts. Instead of ridiculing the idea Jesus actually decided to run with it. Crazy or what? Jesus gave thanks to God for the food and then sent His team off to feed the crowd. As if that doesn't sound crazy enough, listen up to what happened next. The Bible says that everyone had enough to fill their faces (or something like that).

If you want to know how this crazy day ended, then look it up in Bible book John, chapter 6 and verses 12 and 13.

NATIONAL DISTRIBUTORS

UK: (and countries not listed below)
CWR, Waverley Abbey House, Waverley Lane, Farnham, Surrey GU9 8EP.
Tel: (01252) 784700 Outside UK (44) 1252 784700 Email: mail@cwr.org.uk

AUSTRALIA: KI Entertainment, Unit 21 317-321 Woodpark Road, Smithfield, New South Wales 2164. Tel: 1 800 850 777 Fax: 02 9604 3699
Email: sales@kientertainment.com.au

CANADA: David C Cook Distribution Canada, PO Box 98, 55 Woodslee Avenue, Paris, Ontario N3L 3E5. Tel: 1800 263 2664 Email: swansons@cook.ca

GHANA: Challenge Enterprises of Ghana, PO Box 5723, Accra.
Tel: (021) 222437/223249 Fax: (021) 226227 Email: ceg@africaonline.com.gh

HONG KONG: Cross Communications Ltd, 1/F, 562A Nathan Road, Kowloon.
Tel: 2780 1188 Fax: 2770 6229 Email: cross@crosshk.com

INDIA: Crystal Communications, 10-3-18/4/1, East Marredpalli, Secunderabad – 500026, Andhra Pradesh. Tel/Fax: (040) 27737145
Email: crystal_edwj@rediffmail.com

KENYA: Keswick Books and Gifts Ltd, PO Box 10242-00400, Nairobi.
Tel: (254) 20 312639/3870125 Email: keswick@swiftkenya.com

MALAYSIA: Canaanland, No. 25 Jalan PJU 1A/41B, NZX Commercial Centre, Ara Jaya, 47301 Petaling Jaya, Selangor. Tel: (03) 7885 0540/1/2
Fax: (03) 7885 0545 Email: info@canaanland.com.my

Salvation Book Centre (M) Sdn Bhd, 23 Jalan SS 2/64, 47300 Petaling Jaya, Selangor.
Tel: (03) 78766411/78766797 Fax: (03) 78757066/78756360
Email: info@salvationbookcentre.com

NEW ZEALAND: KI Entertainment, Unit 21 317-321 Woodpark Road, Smithfield, New South Wales 2164, Australia. Tel: 0 800 850 777
Fax: +612 9604 3699 Email: sales@kientertainment.com.au

NIGERIA: FBFM, Helen Baugh House, 96 St Finbarr's College Road, Akoka, Lagos.
Tel: (01) 7747429/4700218/825775/827264 Email: fbfm@hyperia.com

PHILIPPINES: OMF Literature Inc, 776 Boni Avenue, Mandaluyong City.
Tel: (02) 531 2183 Fax: (02) 531 1960 Email: gloadlaon@omflit.com

SINGAPORE: Alby Commercial Enterprises Pte Ltd, 95 Kallang Avenue #04-00, AIS Industrial Building, 339420. Tel: (65) 629 27238
Fax: (65) 629 27235 Email: marketing@alby.com.sg

SOUTH AFRICA: Struik Christian Books, 80 MacKenzie Street, PO Box 1144, Cape Town 8000. Tel: (021) 462 4360 Fax: (021) 461 3612
Email: info@struikchristianmedia.co.za

SRI LANKA: Christombu Publications (Pvt) Ltd, Bartleet House, 65 Braybrooke Place, Colombo 2. Tel: (9411) 2421073/2447665
Email: dhanad@bartleet.com

USA: David C Cook Distribution Canada, PO Box 98, 55 Woodslee Avenue, Paris, Ontario N3L 3E5, Canada. Tel: 1800 263 2664 Email: swansons@cook.ca

CWR is a Registered Charity – Number 294387

CWR is a Limited Company registered in England – Registration Number 1990308

More of Andy Robb's colourful Bible stories with crazy cartoons and cliff-hanger endings, to stop you getting bored!

50 Goriest Bible Stories

A sword plunged to the hilt into a super-fat king's blubber, a bloke getting killed by lightning, cold-blooded murder, tons of people drowning, scary skin diseases, famines, earthquakes! Ready to be grossed out? Jump in!

ISBN: 978-1-85345-530-8

50 Wildest Bible Stories

A slippery serpent suggested sin, a bunch of builders babbled away, a pair of past-it parents produced a baby, angels ate with a guy called Abe, bad boys became bear bait! Looking for a really wild time? Tuck in!

ISBN: 978-1-85345-529-2

50 Weirdest Bible Stories

Discover fifty of the weirdest things that happened in the Bible including the crossing of the Red Sea, Jesus healing a paralysed man, heavenly bread in the desert, the strange dreams of Joseph, Peter walking on water and many more. Want some weirdness? Go for it!

ISBN: 978-1-85345-489-9

For current prices visit www.cwr.org.uk

Get into God's Word

Topz is a popular bimonthly devotional for 7- to 11-year-olds.

The Topz Gang teach children biblical truths through daily Bible readings, word games, puzzles, riddles, cartoons, competitions and simple prayers.

Only **£2.75** each
or **£14.95** (UK) for a year's subscription (six issues)

YP's is a dynamic bimonthly devotional for 11- to 15-year-olds.

Each issue is packed with cool graphics, special features and articles, plus daily Bible readings and notes for two months.

Only **£2.75** each
or **£14.95** (UK) for a year's subscription (six issues)

Prices correct at time of printing and exclusive of p&p

Learn about

Danny's Daring Days

Talented footballer Danny learns how to step out in faith, believing that God and His love will always be with him.

ISBN: 978-1-85345-502-5

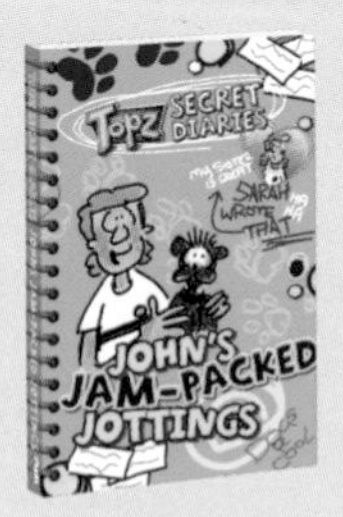

John's Jam-Packed Jottings

John learns about loyalty to Jesus and God's forgiving nature.

ISBN: 978-1-85345-503-2

Josie's Jazzy Journal

Josie, with the help of best friend Sarah, learns how to show God's love.

ISBN: 978-1-85345-457-8

Paul's Potty Pages

Paul from the Topz Gang tries to impress the new American girl in his class, with disastrous results!

ISBN: 978-1-85345-456-1

Benny's Barmy Bits

Discover with Benny how God wants to be the most important part of our lives.

ISBN: 978-1-85345-431-8

Sarah's Secret Scribblings

Join Sarah from the Topz Gang as she learns to pray for people who upset her, discovers that everyone is special to God, and more.

ISBN: 978-1-85345-432-5

Dave's Dizzy Doodles

Dave discovers it's never too late for God to turn things around.

ISBN: 978-1-85345-552-0

Gruff & Saucy's Topzy-Turvy Tales

Gruff and Saucy learn that, although it's sometimes hard trying to live God's way, He gives us the Holy Spirit to help us.

ISBN: 978-1-85345-553-7